THE Abbey-Forge
COOKBOOK
FEEDING FRIENDS AND FAMILY
Sarah Xhumrri

Foreword

Entertaining should be fun.
I have a passion for using quality ingredients to create delicious meals to share with family and friends. No fuss, no panic, just delicious food to share.

Being a busy mum, wife, restaurateur and something of a food evangelist, I know how hard it can be to fit great meals around a busy lifestyle. My recipes have been designed to be fun and easy to follow and allow you to spend as much or as little time as you want creating the perfect get together. By giving you hints and tips that I use in my own restaurants, I know you'll be able to spend less time in the kitchen but still be able to serve up an impressive feast. I'll also give you ideas for table decorations, wine

pairings and cocktail recipes to add those special touches.

Living on the Isle of Man allows us to use the finest fresh, local produce to create fabulous meals for the Abbey and the Forge, and I encourage you to do the same wherever you live. Being the premier wedding and events location on the Island, the Abbey is known for its quality and attention to detail, something which I hope to have brought to the menus in this book. The Forge, which is the only smokehouse and grill on the Isle of Man, serving authentic, fresh dishes, brings inspiration for the hearty, slow-cooked fare found within these covers.

It gives me great pleasure to be able to put this book together. I hope you enjoy it!

Sarah Xhumrri

Lily Publications
Published by **Lily Publications Ltd.**,
PO Box 33, Ramsey, Isle of Man, IM99 4LP
Tel: +44 (0)1624 898446, Fax: +44 (0)1624 898449 www.lilypublications.co.uk lilypubs@manx.net

Acknowledgements

'd like to thank Miles Cowsill and Sara Donaldson for their editorial help, Andrew Lowe for his design and Simon Park and Robyn Ackron for their photography.

Thanks also to my husband Artan, my gorgeous children Dora, Ruben, Edie and Alban, my ever supporting family, dear friends and wonderful clientele.

A special thanks also goes to my most fabulous and dynamic team – always 100% behind even my most abitious projects and, quite frankly, the people who make it all happen.

You know who you are!

Contents

All care and attention should be made to hygiene in food preparation and we advise using the best quality ingredients to obtain the best results.

Consideration should always be given to advising your guests of any possible allergens.

The oven or grill should always be pre-heated to the specified temperature.

Oven temperatures given are for fan-assisted ovens. We recommend using an oven thermometer. If using a non fan-assisted oven, adjust temperatures according to the manufacturer's instructions.

Please see the full advice on page 128.

Introduction

Sarah Xhumrri's first memory is of food. For her, everything revolves around food, wine and family life, and she couldn't be happier...

As she grew up within the hospitality trade, so Sarah's children are an integral part of the business and are pretty handy in the kitchen; ranging from 3 to 10 years of age they are part of the team. With running two successful restaurants, there's no such thing as 'free time' for Sarah, it's a concept that seems alien to her – when she's not at the Abbey or the Forge, she can be found in her vegetable patch or tending to her chickens with her family and her dog. She loves her life and is very proud of what she has achieved both personally and professionally.

Talking to Sarah, you can see she has a knack for understanding her customers' tastes and preferences, and she also never writes down an order. She has the uncanny ability of being able to tell what a diner is going to order before they've even

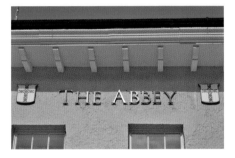

looked at the menu. Such knowledge has come about from a lifetime of working with food and the passion that drives her business. Even as both restaurants have had their fair share of famous visitors, Sarah remains down-to-earth and never divulges secrets.

The Albanian connection

When asked about the most obscure restaurant she has come upon in her travels, she notes that it was in Albania. Restaurants nestled off the beaten track serve the freshest of fresh ingredients – less a question of food miles as yards. Without local knowledge, such as that of her husband Artan, she doubts many people would find such great, hidden eateries. With one of the best chefs in the world, Danish chef René Redzepi, co-owner of the two-

Michelin starred restaurant Noma in Copenhagen, having Albanian ancestry, Sarah reckons that the country will soon be recognised for its fresh, tantalising cuisine. But with her mother-in-law's influence flowing through the pages of this book, and Sarah's love for excellent authentic food, the same emphasis on homemade, fresh and flavoursome recipes can be found in less hard to reach places.

Brought up in Shropshire, Sarah was raised in a country club hotel on the Welsh Borders. She can remember watching, from a young age, as suckling pig and lobsters were prepared for guests – for as long as she can remember she has been surrounded by bakers, fryers, cooks and growers. Her grandmother was a famous baker within the family and, being born and raised in the country club, everyone in her family was connected in some way to the hospitality trade.

Bitten by the bug at a young age, when Sarah was 14 she began work in a local restaurant washing dishes and waiting on tables. Before the foodie

revolution of the late 1990s and early 2000s, she saw how the restaurateur was growing his own produce and raising his own animals for the restaurant.

A love for hospitality

She knew then that the hospitality world was for her. All the way through her A levels, all she could think about was the catering business, so much so that at the age of 17, as soon as she could drive, she was accepted into Llandudno Catering College

– a year early. Sarah continued to work in the same establishment all the way through her catering college years until she opened her own restaurant at the age of 21.

The summer after leaving college, Sarah spent two years in Italy learning her trade and while in Venice, during the summer of 1998, she met her future husband, Artan. With Artan also in the hospitality trade, once she returned home the only thing left to do was open up her own restaurant. She decided to take a risk, walked into her local bank to

Rushen Abbey

ask for a business loan and the rest is history – in 2001 'Gusto', her first establishment, was opened. Sarah's dream had come true as she continued to run the two-storey town centre restaurant serving fresh fish, beautiful salads and local produce. She sold the business in 2005, never having made much money, but gaining valuable experience in the trade.

Artan joined Sarah full-time in 2005 and for a year

Located next to the ancient monastery ruins of Rushen Abbey, the building, built from stone reclaimed from the original abbey in the C18th, was heading towards the end of its life and needed a complete overhaul to bring it back into useful habitation. With a long and varied history as a private house, a boarding school for girls, a country house hotel and at one time housing an award

the couple moved away from the restaurant business to concentrate on property developing. When her parents moved to the Isle of Man, Sarah, now pregnant with their first child, fell in love with the Island and she and Artan decided to also relocate. They moved their business to the Isle of Man at the end of 2006 never expecting that the hospitality industry would again be calling.

Opening the Abbey

After a few years they couldn't resist the temptation to renovate the Abbey, in partnership with Manx National Heritage, and the Abbey as we know it today first opened its doors in 2010.

winning jam factory, the time was right to upgrade and bring it back into use as a restaurant to showcase Sarah and Artan's hospitality.

Today the Abbey, with its four separate spaces (including the garden room, private dining room and two main restaurant areas with a 140-cover dining room), is a stylish, hidden gem nestling next to the monastery ruins. Surrounded by mature trees, and with a babbling stream nearby, the restaurant is the epitome of relaxed country house dining, highlighting the freshest seasonal produce from local artisan makers, farmers and foragers as well as the produce from Sarah's own gardens. To emphasise the seasonality and freshness of the ingredients used at the Abbey, the menu in the 140-cover dining room changes daily to showcase the produce on offer that day.

In keeping with the Abbey's varied history, each of the four areas set aside for dining have their own personality, yet manage to work in perfect harmony. Whether dining in the garden room (where parents can watch their children stay entertained in the outside play area), the two main restaurants, or the private dining room, there is a relaxed sense of comfort and of being well-looked after. The modern European cooking, along with the superb wine list, and the family friendly atmosphere, guarantees that Sarah and Artan's vision of relaxed hospitality is adhered to.

A premier wedding venue

Sarah's passion for the Abbey has also helped to turn it into the premier wedding and events location on the Isle of Man. Abbey weddings are a highly bespoke and individual affair, and events are treated with the upmost privacy and exclusivity. Guests are guaranteed the Abbey's excellent food and drink, and with quality at the very heart of each event the venue is a popular choice for Islanders and visitors alike.

Sarah's attention to detail, and love of her art, really shines through and the Abbey is testimony to what can be achieved through passion and hard work.

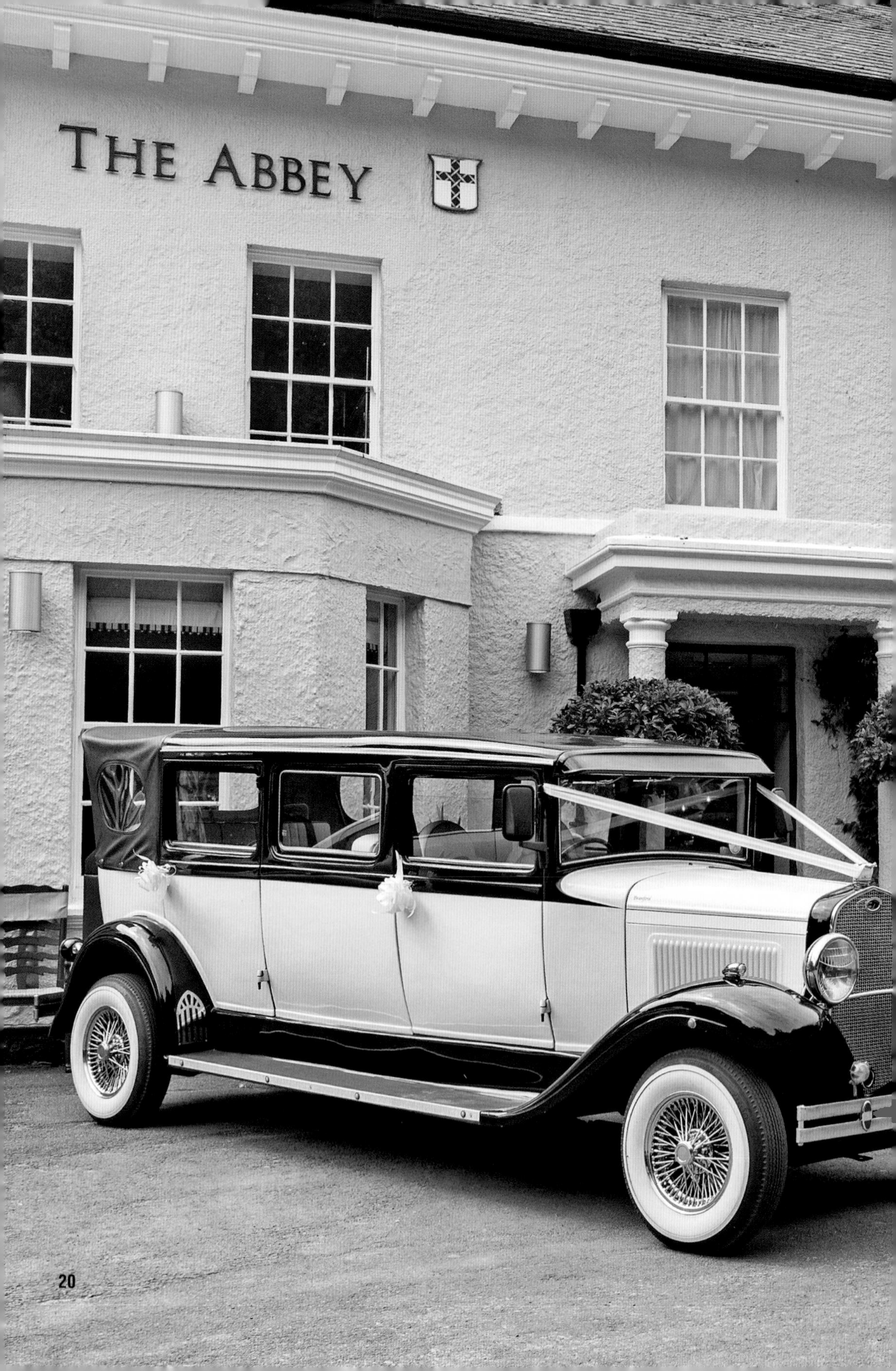
THE ABBEY

FEEDING FRIENDS & FAMILY

A second restaurant beckons

But a few years after opening the Abbey, Sarah and Artan were about to take another huge leap into the unknown. The Forge was a location that Sarah had fallen in love with. Since their arrival on the Island the couple had always said that if the property came on the market they would purchase it – and when the call eventually came from the owner they said yes right away. It was destined to be their second restaurant.

A few days after acquiring the keys, in the spring of 2013, the now famous snow storms hit the Isle of Man and the Forge was only accessible by the couple leaving their car some way off and sliding down to the building from the roadside. It was then that they realised, despite the fact that they'd reached their financial limits on a dilapidated old Manx farm with a caved-in roof, that the site was something special and should remain true to its authentic Manx history. With the enforced closure, they saw the

All our Products
are freshly made
with LOVE!

♥ TAKE AWAY
A TREAT

COTO D

For
U
Beyon
Rang

THE FORGE

24 THE FORGE
MERINGUE

Food Festival 2017

potential in the beautiful grounds and surroundings and decided to strip the building back to its original state. Using old fixtures and fittings that they discovered on-site, they respectfully restored the interior, and even found slate fireplace mantels hidden beneath the old front porch. Now, with large open-plan dining rooms and crackling fires when the seasons turn cold, the Forge is unique to the Isle of Man as a smokehouse and grill, serving authentic, fresh dishes based around the couple's Albanian and British market town roots.

When visitors eat at the Forge Smokehouse and Grill, they can look forward to leisurely family-style feasting on homemade dishes made from scratch on-site. Sarah uses the best meat, fish and vegetables, which are marinated, slow-cooked and dressed in the house's own secret seasoning. Keeping the food miles low, the couple grows as much of their own produce as possible, and even the ketchup, butter and condiments are homemade. As with the Abbey, Sarah keeps an outstanding wine list to accompany the food, sourcing Own Label house

The best of local produce

From that first love of the building, to today's popular restaurant, what could so easily have been a mistake has proved to be a testimony to Sarah and Artan's determination to do what they love, and love what they do. As with the Abbey, they support the local farmers and food producers, working closely with them to offer their customers the very best slow-cooked, tasty, quality food.

wines that perfectly balance with the dishes on offer. There are even botanical, crafted cocktails and infusions for the adventurous diner.

So, now, after 11 years on the Island, Sarah and Artan are happily running two restaurants and bringing up a family doing what they love – bringing the very best in hospitality to those around them and showcasing what can be achieved with fresh, local, top-quality produce.

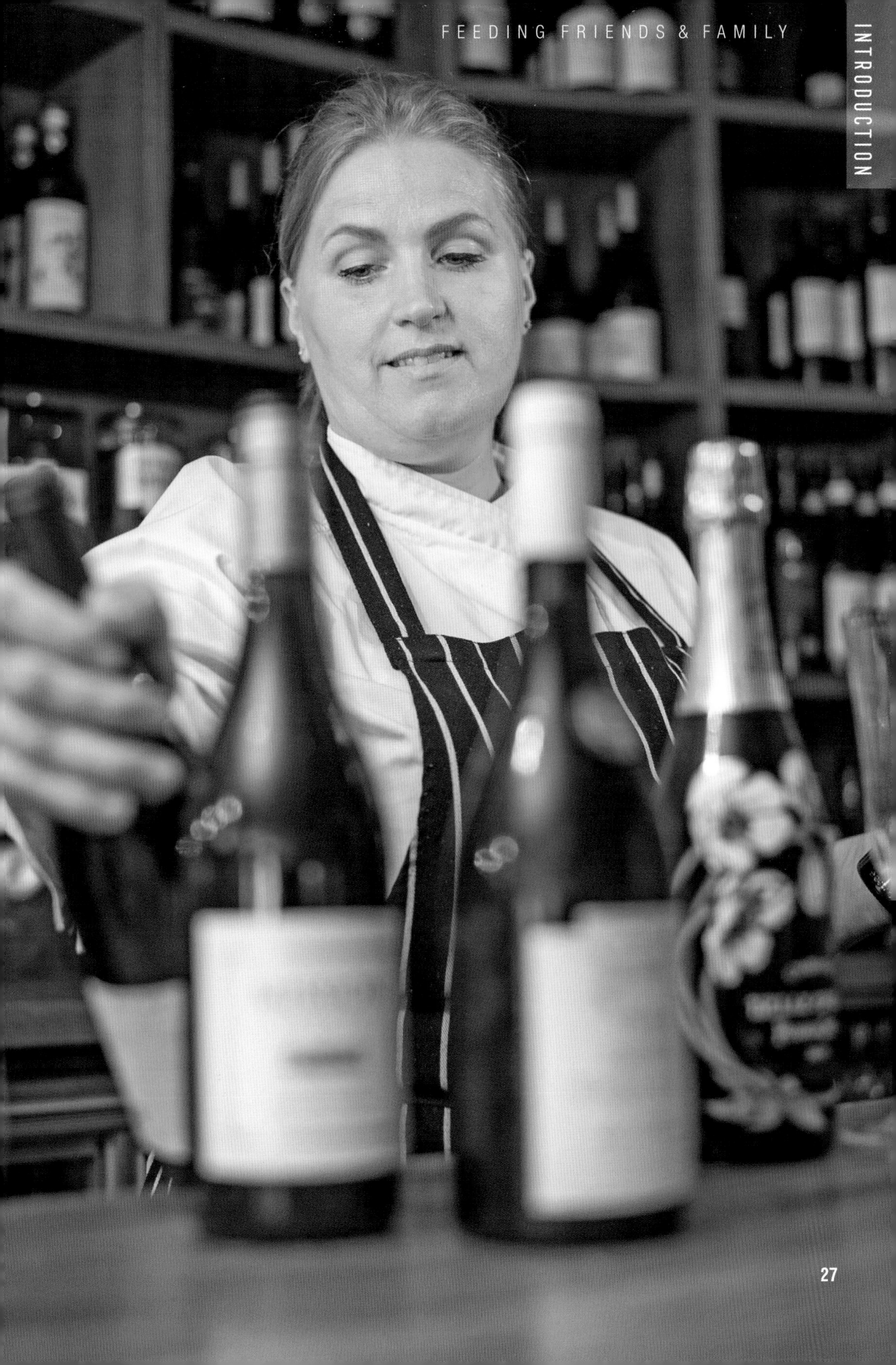

Island Suppliers

Living on an island can prove difficult when sourcing supplies for any business: what cannot be grown or made at home has to be shipped in, and can be costly. Artisan suppliers were thin on the ground when Sarah and Artan first opened the Abbey, however, the artisan food sector has been revolutionised in the last 10 years and home-grown produce on the Isle of Man has flourished, with first-class meat, fish and vegetables available all year round ...

Robinson's, one of the oldest family businesses on the Isle of Man, helps supply the Abbey and the Forge with the freshest produce possible. Committed to supporting the growers and producers of the Island, their core objectives fit well with Sarah's principles of wanting to showcase the best the Island has to offer. Local flour, oil, meat, confectionery, dairy and vegetable producers all work with the firm to distribute their products.

For an Island renowned for its fresh, top-quality seafood, Sarah is spoilt for choice when it comes to fish. **Cushlin Seafood** keeps the restaurants supplied with the freshest of local fish and seafood, including lobster and the famous Manx scallops, while Robinsons handle the large wet fish supply.

The **Isle of Man Creamery** ensures that the Abbey and Forge are supplied with first-class dairy products. The Island has long been famed for its award-winning

Local butcher **Harrison & Garrett** take the very best of care in the restaurant supply, and both restaurants are proud to use beef, pork and lamb from Ballaloaghtan farm – a rare-breeds farm only four miles away from the Abbey. Part of the organic slow-food movement the farm is reintroducing rare breeds all under grass-fed natural conditions. It's reassuring for Sarah to know exactly where her meat comes from and she can see the quality of care the animals receive first-hand. The quality is definitely of the high standard required by the Abbey and Forge.

Staarvey Farm supply Sarah's salads and organic herbs, shoots and vegetables.

cheese and the creamery, a small co-operative of the Island's family-owned dairy producers, is dedicated to reflecting the culinary heritage and traditional cheese-making skills of the Isle of Man in its products. Isle of Man cheese and cream is second to none. They also deliver **Gelling free-range eggs** on a daily basis.

For making those beautiful pies and pastries, Sarah relies on local artisan flours. **Laxey Glen Flour Mill** provides a wide variety of flours produced on the Island from locally grown Manx milling wheat. When creating meals for the restaurants the team can use Isle of Man produce with nothing appearing from off the Island.

And it's not just the food that's home-grown. Beers used at the Abbey and the Forge come from **Bushy's Brewery** and local distributors **Heron & Brearley**. **Bushy's** has been brewing for over 30 years now, since its first brew beneath the old Bushy's pub in Victoria Street, Douglas in 1985, moving to its first brewery building at Mount Murray in 1990. Producing bitter, stout and mild, Bushy's championed the retention of the Isle of Man's historic Pure Beer Act in 1995, ensuring that only the purest of ingredients are used to make beer and ale on the Island.

As for the wines … these are sourced worldwide, and when Sarah isn't at work she often sources the wines herself on trips abroad. Ensuring that the wines served complement the food is important and, as with the dishes prepared in the Abbey and the Forge, only the best will do.

THE FISH

FRESH FISH &

Flowers

Big and bold. Think lily or sunflowers – something to wake up to in the morning.

Table dressing

Frilly or plaid tablecloths; fork, knife and spoon rolled in napkins; salt and pepper; butter and toast; a side plate and butter knife.

BREAKFAST

If you're lucky enough to have time for a leisurely breakfast, then make the most of it!

Pile the table high with everything you might need and don't move for an hour or so...

sublime!

BREAKFAST DRINKS

Of course there should always be freshly squeezed orange juice and brewed coffee...

BREAKFAST COCKTAIL

...but when it comes to matching booze to your breakfast then you can't go far wrong with a classic Buck's Fizz. However, in the world of catering there is always an occasion that calls for something stronger, so I've included something for times such as those.

Serves 1

Breakfast Martini

We created this variation of the classic at our restaurant, the Forge, when we were asked to cater a very special breakfast celebration. Our mixologist spent around a week infusing the fruits and vodka. It could very easily be made with fruit purées instead, which would also stem the alcohol consumption!

INGREDIENTS

50ml breakfast vodka mix (see below)
25ml triple sec / Cointreau
50ml orange juice
50ml mango juice

METHOD

Add all the ingredients to a shaker filled with ice and shake until well chilled.

Double strain into a Martini glass and garnish with a dried orange slice.

Breakfast Vodka Mix

INGREDIENTS

1 whole ripe pineapple
1 large ripe mango
700ml vodka

METHOD

Peel and chop both the mango and pineapple into chunks and place in mason jar. Top with vodka, seal, leave for approximately 5–12 days in a cool place and give it a good shake every day.

Abbey Eggs

INGREDIENTS

4 English breakfast muffins
8 eggs (soft poached, 4 mins)
400g spinach (wilted)
butter (for spreading)

Hollandaise Sauce

2 egg yolks
1 tbsp lemon juice
1 tsp Dijon mustard
100g butter (melted)

To serve

truffle oil
freshly ground black pepper

METHOD

Prep time: 5 minutes   Cook time: 20 minutes

For the Hollandaise Sauce

Set the yolks, lemon juice and mustard in a bowl over a pan of simmering water and whisk well. Gradually pour in the melted butter, whisking briskly all the time until all the butter is emulsified into the yolk mixture.

For the Muffins

Slice the muffins in half and toast them. Butter them and place 2 pieces per guest on the plate

Top the muffins with spinach wilted quickly in a warm pan.

Carefully place an egg, on top of the spinach, on each slice of muffin and cover with hollandaise sauce.

To Serve

Drizzle with white truffle oil and black pepper.

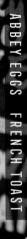

Serves 6

French Toast

One of my children's most favourite breakfast treats: less mess than pancakes and just as much fun to flip in a pan! You can pile them with fruits and berries or be naughty and dollop a lump of crunchy peanut butter and good quality maple syrup – absolute indulgence – yum.

INGREDIENTS

4 beaten eggs
1 tbsp of caster sugar
½ tsp of ground cinnamon
pinch of freshly ground nutmeg
100ml double cream (or milk if you prefer)

12 thick slices of white bread (crusts removed)
butter for frying

To serve

your favourite toppings
icing sugar for dusting

METHOD

Prep time: 5 minutes   Cook time: 15 minutes

Mix the eggs, sugar, spices, and double cream together in a bowl then tip in to a deepish baking tray.

Lay the bread slices onto the egg mixture for around 30 seconds and then flip the bread over and allow time for the mixture to soak into the bread.

Heat a knob of butter in a non-stick frying pan until the butter smokes just a little. Place the bread slices into the pan a few at a time – most pans fit 2

or 3 slices at a time. Fry until golden brown and flip over on to the other side and repeat.

To Serve

Once cooked, pile high on a plate and top with your chosen topping.

To finish dredge heavily with icing sugar from a sieve or sugar dredger.

Serves 4

Ham and Potatoes

INGREDIENTS

2 ham hocks
1 large white onion
2 carrots
1 orange
2 bay leaves
10 whole cloves
1 stick cinnamon
2 celery sticks
6 large potatoes
2 tbsp flat leaf parsley (chopped)
1 tbsp wholegrain mustard

To Serve

best olive oil
freshly ground black pepper
crusty bread

METHOD

Prep time: 15 minutes   Cook time: 4 hours

Place the ham hocks into a deep saucepan along with everything (roughly chopped) apart from the parsley, mustard and potatoes. Cover the ingredients with cold water and bring to the boil.

Once simmering, turn down the heat and simmer for 2–4 hours until the ham is easy to push off the bone.

As the ham is simmering, peel and chop the potatoes and boil in salted water until tender. Drain and allow to dry off in a colander.

Remove the ham hock from the liquid and shred the meat up, then put into a large mixing bowl, add the potatoes, chopped parsley and wholegrain mustard and mix well.

To Serve

To serve drizzle with fresh olive oil and pepper and serve with warm crusty bread. The stock from the ham can be strained off and used for making a delicious pea and ham soup.

Serves 4

Homemade Yoghurt

So simple and such a natural and delicious flavour. I first saw this, along with butter making, when I visited my mother-in-law in Albania. Each day a litre of unpasteurized milk is delivered to her door and in the early hours she sets about making her butter, yoghurt and milk for the day. Such simple things that are so delicious and really make a difference to the food she produces.

I started making this regularly because in a house with four children, I would often find that the yoghurt pot was almost empty at night as I planned for the next day, and we simply can't do without yoghurt at breakfast time in our house. You can add all the usual things – fruit, nuts, seeds and honey and the great thing is the yoghurt doesn't contain any fillers, thickener or any of the additives you see in many yoghurts in the supermarket – even in plain yoghurt sometimes!

You will need to have very clean utensils but nothing too complicated is needed.

INGREDIENTS

568ml (1 pt) whole milk
1 tbsp of your favourite natural yoghurt (must contain cultures or be 'live')

METHOD

Prep time: 20 minutes   Setting time: 4 hours min

Warm the milk to just below boiling point, stir the milk gently as it heats to make sure the bottom doesn't scorch and the milk doesn't boil over.

Let the milk cool until it is warm to the touch – about 40°C. Stir occasionally to prevent a skin from forming.

Scoop out a ladleful of warm milk and add it to the yoghurt. Whisk until smooth and the yoghurt is dissolved in the milk.

Pour the thinned yoghurt into the warm milk while whisking gently.

Put the pot of warm yoghurt/milk mixture in a warm place – airing cupboard, oven that has been pre-heated to 150°C then switched off or a warm spot in the house – I keep mine in the cupboard next to the fridge that is always warm.

Let the yoghurt set for at least 4 hours or as long as overnight — the exact time will depend on the cultures used, the temperature of the yoghurt, and your yoghurt preferences. The longer yoghurt sits the thicker and more tart it becomes.

Once the yoghurt has set to your liking, remove it from the warm place. Water, called whey, will be all around the yoghurt – you can either stir it in or drain it off (my husband drinks it and swears by its nutritional goodness). Transfer to storage containers, cover, and refrigerate. Homemade yoghurt will keep for about 2 weeks in the refrigerator.

Once you start making your own yoghurt, you can use some of each batch to culture your next batch.

Burek

Another of my mother-in-law's recipes. As a chef I thoroughly enjoy immersing myself in another culture's cuisine and none more than Albanian. So many traditions have been preserved and in most households meals are made from scratch as processed supermarket food is frowned upon.

When I first saw my mother-in-law clear off the kitchen table, and bring out a long, skinny rolling pin and heavy linen cloths, I knew something good was coming. I was then invited to join the other female guest to help with the rolling and stretching of the most exquisite fresh filo pastry I have ever tasted. It is time consuming, and a little messy if you're not a pro, but worth the work.

For this recipe I have included shop bought filo pasty for convenience but, if you have the time, I recommend watching an online video of how to make filo traditionally and giving it a go...

Burek

INGREDIENTS

1 pack shop bought filo pastry
250g spinach (washed and roughly chopped)
1 tbsp fresh dill (chopped)
1 tbsp fresh parsley (chopped)
200g feta cheese
olive oil
salt
freshly ground pepper

To Serve

homemade natural yoghurt

METHOD

Prep time: 5 minutes   Cook time: 35 minutes

Preheat oven to 180ºC/gas 6.

Oil an ovenproof dish of your choice – it will need to be approx. 3 inches (7.5cm) deep.

Lay 1 sheet of filo in the dish, allowing the excess pastry to flop over the sides of the dish and on to the table.

Lightly oil the sheet and place another on top in the opposite direction to create a cross, then repeat in a criss-cross style until all the pastry is used. Remember to oil between each sheet.

Fill the well in the pastry with the chopped spinach, dill and parsley, and crumble on the feta cheese. Season with a little salt and plenty of freshly ground black pepper.

Drizzle with olive oil and begin folding all the flaps of pastry inwards to create a lid for the burek. The sheets may need a little oil on the other side as you go along. Make sure the top of the pie is completely covered in pastry.

Place the burek in the oven for 25–35 minutes until deep golden brown all over.

To Serve

When you take the burek out of the oven allow it to rest for 10 minutes before slicing and serving with homemade natural yoghurt

LIGHT LUNCHEON

As with breakfast, the aim is to stay put when hosting a lunch. All of these recipes can be put on the table a little ahead of time and left there, so that you can sit and enjoy a smashing time catching up with friends or family.

Flowers

Light and fluffy, keep it small and unintimidating.

Table dressing

Fresh mayonnaise and lemon wedges; cutlery rolled in napkins and perhaps a little water – rosé house punch is enough for me.

LIGHT LUNCHEON **WINE MATCH**

When matching wines for lunchtime it's important to consider the weather; as guests arrive will they be coming in through a storm or bright sunshine?

I always feel eating and drinking are so affected by this, and a good all-rounder type white wine will stand you in good stead for the beginning of a light lunch: something light for sure, and usually with a citrus ilk as it will be, perhaps, the first drink of the day for your guests – one hopes!

I am recommending an Albarino from Spain because it fits well with the things we have discussed. Of course, if you happen to know one of your guests has a favourite wine then it is suitable to serve that instead.

Red wine may not be needed over lunch depending on the length of lunch, and of course your guest list, but it's always handy to have something prepared just in case.

It's important to keep it light once again and to choose something that won't overpower the light food on offer... I've plumped for a New Zealand Pinot Noir because it's great with the duck leg and beef, and still light enough all round.

LIGHT LUNCHEON **COCKTAIL**
Serves 4

House Rosé Punch

This was originally designed in-house using red wine and is a huge seller, especially through the summer months. However, we have adapted it for this book to use the rosé wine which makes for a lighter option and looks so tempting! If you're ever passing the Forge then pop in and try out its big brother 'house punch'.

INGREDIENTS

fresh cucumber (sliced)
fresh strawberries
fresh raspberries
25ml peach purée
250ml elderflower pressé
half a bottle of rosé wine
100ml gin
fresh mint leaves
25ml fresh lime juice

METHOD

Add all the fresh fruits to a jug (approx. 1 litre) then add all the other ingredients.

Top with ice and stir well.

Serves 6

Duck Leg Confit

INGREDIENTS

6 duck legs
20g sea salt
20g Chinese five-spice powder
20 peppercorns
8 pieces star anise
6 cinnamon sticks
4 bay leaves

1 garlic bulb (chopped in half, skin on)
1 ltr vegetable oil / duck fat to cover

To Serve

Red onion marmalade
dauphinoise potatoes (pg. 118)
crusty bread
peppery salad

METHOD

Prep time: 5 minutes   Cook time: 4 hours
Preheat oven to 150ºC/gas 4

Rub the duck legs with the salt and Chinese
five-spice and place in a deep ovenproof dish.

Sprinkle the other ingredients over the legs and then
cover with the oil or duck fat.

Cover with greaseproof paper and foil and place into
the oven at 150ºC for 4 hours.

Remove from the oil and grill for 5 minutes
before serving.

Catering Cheats

Sieve the leftover oil and keep in the freezer ready for
future use in confit or for the best roasties ever!

To Serve

Red onion marmalade and dauphinoise potatoes
(pg. 118) or crusty bread and a peppery salad.

Serves 6

Beef Carpaccio

INGREDIENTS

750g cooked beef – left over from either
   Sunday Roast (pg. 76)
   or Blackened Beef (pg. 118)
4 tbsp soy sauce
a few drops of sesame oil
1 lemon (juiced)
2 tbsp best olive oil
500g rocket
150g Parmesan cheese (shaved)

To Serve

1 tbsp sesame seeds
lemon wedges
optional: red chilli (finely chopped)

METHOD

Prep time: 15 minutes   Cook time: 0 minutes

Chill the meat and slice as thinly as possible.

Spread the slices with your fingers onto
a serving platter.

Mix the soy sauce, sesame oil, lemon juice and
olive oil to make the dressing, then set aside.

Sprinkle the rocket and Parmesan cheese over
the beef.

To Serve

Drizzle over the soy dressing and sesame seeds,
then garnish with lemon wedges.

Add some finely chopped red chilli for a more
fiery offering.

Coconut Tempura Prawns

with Avocado Purée

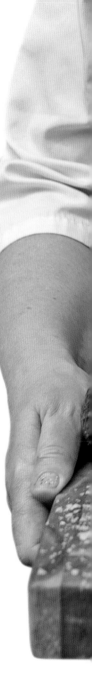

INGREDIENTS

Coconut King Prawn Tempura
Serves 6

500g raw king prawns (peeled)
1 ltr oil
100g flour
100g cornflour
50g desiccated coconut
½ tsp chilli flakes
285ml soda water (chilled, or sparkling
   water with a little baking soda added)
zest and juice of 1 lime
a few drops of sesame oil
a pinch of salt

Avocado Purée
Serves 6–8

4 ripe avocados
1 green chilli
2 tbsp coriander (chopped)
juice of 1 lime
salt

To Serve

chilli sauce
fresh lime wedges
a sprinkle of coriander

METHOD

For the King Prawns:
Prep time 10 minutes
Cook time 6 minutes

For the Avocado Purée:
Prep time 10 minutes
Cook time 0 minutes

**For the Coconut
King Prawn Tempura**

Butterfly all of the prawns
(slice almost in half lengthways)
and leave to dry off on a tea towel.

Heat the oil in a deep pan, to about
180ºC, ready to fry the prawns.

Mix all the dry ingredients well, then add
the lime juice and zest, and the drops of
sesame oil. Whisk in the water
a little at a time to create a thick batter.

Coat each prawn gently in the batter and
place into the hot oil to fry until golden.

Fry small amounts at a time to make sure
they do not stick together, and set on a tea
towel to drain as you fry the rest.

For the Avocado Purée

Blend all of the ingredients together in
a food processor and serve.

Cover the purée when not in use, as it
will discolour otherwise.

To Serve

Serve the prawns with chilli sauce, fresh
lime wedges, a sprinkle of coriander and the
avocado purée.

Serves 6

Asparagus Tart

INGREDIENTS

Short crust pastry
– approx. 400g
(or shop bought is fine!)

250g plain flour
110g cold butter (diced)
2 tbsp water
pinch of salt

Filling

500g asparagus (chopped)
4 eggs
200ml double cream
150g Parmesan cheese (grated)
1 tbsp parsley (chopped)
1 tbsp mint (chopped)
2 tbsp spring onion (chopped)
salt and pepper

To Serve

salad
crème fraiche

METHOD

Prep time: 30 minutes   Cook time: 1½ hours

For the Pastry

Blitz the flour, butter and salt in a food processor until it resembles breadcrumbs.

Add the cold water a little at a time until the pastry mix forms.

Wrap in cling film and chill for 30 minutes

For the Tart

Preheat oven to 170°C/gas 5

Roll out the pastry and line a greased 25.5cm (10") fluted tart case.

Place the pastry into the case, tapping down to ensure that it fits snugly. Chill in the fridge while you prepare the rest of the ingredients.

Once chilled, line the pastry with baking parchment and fill with either ceramic baking beans or dried pulses, then blind bake the tart case in the pre-heated oven for 20 minutes at 170°C.

Mix all the remaining ingredients together and season well with salt and pepper.

After 20 minutes carefully remove the baking beans and parchment, then pour the mixture into the pastry case. Cook at 170°C for a further 45 minutes until golden and slightly firm to the touch.

To Serve

Salad and crème fraiche, ideally eaten straight away, but this tart will chill well and is just as delicious cold!

Meringues

Makes 2 Pavlova sized ones, 12 large ones or lots of little ones ...

INGREDIENTS

12 egg whites
680g granulated sugar
colourings and flavourings of your choice

To Serve

double cream (whipped)
fresh fruit

METHOD

Prep time: 20 minutes   Cook time: 2–4 hours

Preheat oven to 110ºC/gas ½

Whisk the egg whites until stiff using
a kitchen mixer.

Gradually pour in all of the sugar and continue to mix on a high speed until smooth and glossy (about 8 minutes).

Add a few drops of your chosen flavouring and colouring to taste, and mix again for 1 minute.

Spoon the mixture onto a greaseproof-paper lined tray in the desired shape and size (a piping bag will also work well).

Turn the oven down to 90ºC/gas ¼ .

Cook in the oven for roughly 2–4 hours (depending on the size of the meringues) until completely crisp.

Store in an airtight container and use to impress guests whenever necessary (or just treat yourself...).

To Serve

Lashings of whipped double cream and fresh fruits.

AFTERNOON TEA

At the Abbey we serve afternoon tea every afternoon and it's always a special event. There is nothing quite like taking a whole afternoon out for a tea-sipping, cake-eating catch up with friends. Since opening in 2010 the Abbey has used over 130,000 Manx eggs: most of those in our pastry section making all the ice cream, cakes and egg sandwiches served in the afternoons.

The devil is in the detail on this one, where delicacy and opulence are both called for. Add some extra treats or little chocolates to build an afternoon to remember.

Table dressing

When preparing for an afternoon tea, lay out your finest china cups and teapot (loose-leaf tea adds a little old school glamour) and perhaps a coffee pot if you know a guest may prefer it.

The table can be prepared well in advance leaving you time on the day to finish off by adding milk and sugar, butter and cream, fresh fruit such as strawberries, figs and grapes, fresh flowers, and tea strainers. Linen napkins – a must!

AFTERNOON TEA **WINE MATCH**

Champagne

Nothing sets the scene for a sparkling afternoon tea quite like a glass of something sparkly!

Champagne, with its biscuity crispness is the perfect start and will open everyone's appetite for a long afternoon of indulgence.

Prosecco and cava will also work and friends of mine love to pimp up their fizz with syrups such as elderflower or cassis.

AFTERNOON TEA **COCKTAIL**

Serves 1

Rhubarb Fizz

I have chosen this cocktail to serve with afternoon tea as it embodies the 'Englishness' of tea taking, and when I taste this it reminds me of my grandfather's wonderful summer rose garden where my love for cucumber sandwiches and meringue (my granny was the best baker I have ever met) began.

INGREDIENTS

25ml gin
25ml rhubarb syrup
10ml fresh lemon juice
Champagne / Prosecco

METHOD

Add the gin, rhubarb syrup and lemon juice to a shaker and dry shake (no ice).

Pour into a champagne flute, top with champagne or Prosecco and ...

... enjoy!

Delicate Finger Sandwiches

INGREDIENTS

your favourite sandwich bread
  (4 slices per guest)
butter

Various Fillings

cheese
ham
egg mayonnaise
smoked salmon
coronation chicken
cucumber (essential!)
prawn Marie Rose
cream cheese

To Serve

pickles
chutney
fresh herbs

METHOD

Prep time: 20 minutes   Cook time: 0 minutes

Always butter your bread to help keep the moisture from any fillings away from the bread.

Fill each sandwich and stack them up in piles of 4 or 5, taking care to alternate fillings (e.g. ham, egg, cheese...).

Hold the pile firmly with one hand and trim the crusts off carefully with a sharp, serrated knife.

Slice the pile into 3 sections, creating 3 finger sandwich sections with one of each filling included.

To Serve

Garnish with pickles, chutney and fresh herbs.

Makes 6

Scones

One of the Abbey's most iconic recipes and many clients visit us weekly to enjoy a freshly baked scone.

Up until opening the Abbey in 2010 my scones often resembled something more akin to a fallen meteorite than the fluffy scone I bake today and that is down to the Abbey's long-serving pastry chef, Michael Potts, who taught me this fail-safe recipe and I have been baking them ever since!

INGREDIENTS

Scones

110g sugar
110g butter
450g self-raising flour
250ml buttermilk

Glaze

2 tbsp cream
2 tbsp sugar

To Serve

jam (the best you can get)
cream (whipped or clotted)

METHOD

Prep time: 15 minutes   Cook time: 25 minutes

Preheat oven to 170°C/gas 5

Place the sugar and butter into a food processor and blend until smooth. Next add the self-raising flour and blend again to form breadcrumbs.

While the mixture is still blending, slowly add the buttermilk and keep blending until the mixture is combined and comes away from the sides of the bowl.

Remove your scones from the mixer and shape into a ball (fruit or chocolate can be added at this stage).

Turn out onto a lightly-floured surface and press down on the dough to create a flat circle ready to cut out your scones. The dough should be 5cm thick.

Use a pastry cutter to cut out the scones and place them on a baking sheet lined with greaseproof paper.

For the Glaze

Mix the cream and sugar to make a thick glaze and cover the tops of the scones before putting them in the oven for 22 minutes.

Check the oven after 18 minutes and adjust the timer if necessary.

When ready your scones should be a pale golden colour and well-risen.

To Serve

Always serve with the best jam you can get your hands on, butter and lashings of whipped or clotted cream.

Victoria Sandwich

INGREDIENTS

Sponge

226g sugar
226g margarine – yes, margarine!
  Your cake will be light and fluffy
  and will last for days
  (depending on
  who's around!)
226g self-raising flour
4 eggs
6 drops of vanilla essence
  or the seeds of
  a vanilla pod

To Serve

double cream (whipped)
jam of your choice

METHOD

Prep time: 15 minutes   Cook time: 35 minutes

Dressing: 10 minutes

Preheat oven to 170ºC/gas 5

Add all the ingredients to an electric mixer and beat until smooth (8–10 minutes).

While the batter is mixing, line a 20cm (8") cake tin with greaseproof paper.

Place the sponge mixture into the cake tin and place in the oven for 25 minutes.

Check to see if the cake is done by pushing a skewer through the centre, it should come out clean when fully cooked. This may take up to an extra 10 minutes.

To Serve

Lashings of whipped double cream and homemade jam.

Bakewell Tart

INGREDIENTS

Shortcrust Pastry

225g plain flour (with extra for dusting)
150g butter (with extra for greasing)
25g icing sugar
2 egg yolks

Filling

225g butter
225g sugar
3 eggs
3 egg yolks
almond essence – a few drops to taste
180g ground almonds
120g plain flour
6 tbsp jam – enough to cover the bottom of the tart.
   Raspberry is my favourite, but anything will do

To Serve

double cream

METHOD

Prep time: 30 minutes Cook time: 60–80 minutes

Preheat oven to 170ºC/gas 5

For the Pastry

For the shortcrust pastry, combine all of the ingredients in a food processor until the mixture becomes a smooth paste.

Grease a 20cm (8") fluted tart case with butter, then dust with plain flour.

Smooth the pastry into the tart case and smooth it out with your fingertips (this pastry is far too crumbly to roll out!).

Chill in the fridge for 30 minutes while you get everything else ready.

For the Filling

Cream the butter and sugar together, and then add the eggs, yolks and almond essence. Next, slowly add the ground almonds and plain flour.

To Create the Tart

Line the chilled tart case with baking paper and fill with baking beans, rice or old lentils and bake in the pre-heated oven for up to 20 minutes (blind baking) until golden all over.

Once removed from the oven, cover the base of the tart with a layer of jam.

Add the frangipane filling mixture to the tart on top of the layer of jam carefully a spoonful at a time so as to keep the jam underneath the frangipane to create layers.

Bake in the oven for 40–48 minutes at 170ºC.

To Serve

If you're eating this when it's still warm from the oven, then it's really good with cold double cream. Something that is truly world class here on the Isle of Man is the dairy and none more so than the double cream.

Serves 6–8

Brownie

INGREDIENTS

250g dark chocolate
175g butter
2 eggs
3 egg yolks
275g sugar
110g plain flour
1 tsp instant coffee
1 tsp vanilla extract

To Serve

ice cream
whipped cream

METHOD

Prep time: 20 minutes   Cook time: 40 minutes

Preheat oven to 170ºC/gas 5

Melt the chocolate and butter together in a microwave oven, being careful not to overheat. Stop and stir the mixture every 20 seconds or so to make sure the mixture doesn't burn.

Cream the eggs, yolks and sugar with an electric mixer until light and fluffy. Next, fold the chocolate mixture into the eggs and sugar.

Slowly add the flour, coffee and vanilla extract and mix until all combined.

Line a 20cm (8") baking tray with greaseproof paper and place the brownie mix into the tray.

Cook for 35 minutes at 170ºC.

To Serve

Serve with whipped cream or ice cream for a delicious dessert.

Flowers

Reds and golds, with plenty of candlelight.

Table dressing

Linen napkins; no tablecloth if you don't need one (wooden tables); plenty of condiments; bread and butter; starter, main and dessert cutlery and a bread plate.

Spectacular SUNDAY ROAST

My absolute favourite meal to entertain with – almost everyone who owns a kitchen in the UK knows how much work goes into a Sunday roast and I love to have my friends over to give them an afternoon off!

Of course, I employ all my catering cheats for such an occasion and attempt to pull it off as easily and efficiently as possible.

Most of the dishes can be prepared the day before, so you can have an easy start to your Sunday morning. Most importantly serve a little later in the day ... 2.30 p.m. at the earliest ... let lunch linger on and serve a cheeseboard later when people start to feel peckish again.

SUNDAY ROAST WINE MATCH

Prepare your wines in good time for Sunday lunch: the red can be opened up an hour or so before, and fill an ice bucket with the white and allow to chill down.

Red – Barolo, from Italy. Warming, intense and well balanced. Just right for delicious roast beef. I love to serve Barolo as for the most part they are big wines – not for wimps, and just scream Sunday roast!

White – oaked Chardonnay. I have selected an Australian white here, from the Margaret River region. Many of us are terrified of oaked Chardonnays, but give this a try with the beautiful smoky salmon dish and you won't be disappointed.

SUNDAY ROAST COCKTAILS

In the Forge we're proud to have a pretty extensive Bloody Mary list and we understand that there are a few culinary moments when only a fantastically made Bloody Mary will do! They're boozy, acidic and spicy, which all leads to opening up your guests' appetites for a long afternoon of pretty heavy food...

Serves 1

Classic Bloody Mary

INGREDIENTS

50ml vodka
20ml lemon juice
20ml Bloody Mary Spice Mix
  for a medium spice
  (see below)
100ml tomato juice

To Serve

celery sticks
lemon slices or wedges
freshly ground black pepper

METHOD

Place all the ingredients in a shaker, shake and strain over ice.

Add celery sticks, lemon slices or wedges and freshly ground black pepper as a garnish.

Bloody Mary Spice Mix

For adding to above recipe

INGREDIENTS

1 handful fresh basil
15–20 sprigs fresh thyme
50ml cooking port
1 garlic clove
1 bar spoon salt
1 bar spoon pepper
1 bar spoon horseradish

1 bar spoon
  wholegrain mustard
1 small bottle Tabasco
1 bar spoon smoked paprika
1 fresh chilli
300ml Worcestershire sauce
50ml honey

METHOD

Blend all ingredients well. Taste, and if too spicy top up with more Worcestershire sauce. Bottle up to use when needed for your Classic Bloody Mary.

Serves 6

Home-Smoked Salmon
and Horseradish Cream

INGREDIENTS

Salmon

180g salt
150g sugar
2 lemons (zest and juice)
2 tbsp dill (chopped)
500g freshest salmon (bones removed)

For the Smoking

2 handfuls of smoking chips

Horseradish Cream

good quality horseradish sauce
double cream
salt and pepper

To Serve

lemon wedges
olive oil
freshly ground pepper

METHOD

Prep time: 30 minutes   Chill and smoke time: 7 hours

For the Salmon

Mix the salt, sugar, lemon zest, lemon juice and dill together, and cover the fish in the mixture.

Chill in the fridge, in a plastic or glass container, for a minimum of 6 hours.

Remove from the fridge, rinse well in cold water for 10 minutes then pat dry.

Burn the chips in a pan, allow them to smoulder and place the salmon, on top of a cake rack, above the smouldering wood chips.

Cover the pan tightly with tin foil to seal in the smoke.

Leave for 1 hour, then remove the fish and, when cooled, refrigerate well.

For the Horseradish Cream

Mix the horseradish sauce and cream together until well combined and season to taste.

To Serve

Slice as thinly as you can and serve with horseradish cream, lemon wedges, a drizzle of olive oil and freshly ground black pepper.

Rare Roast Beef

Buy whole sirloin from your butcher and don't worry if you have a little over as this will keep and make great salads and sandwiches all week…

Rare Roast Beef

INGREDIENTS

250g per guest (approx.) sirloin of beef

To Serve

all your favourite vegetables
homemade gravy

METHOD

Prep time: 20 minutes   Cooking time: 8 hours

Preheat oven to 210°C/gas 8

Season the beef heavily with salt and
black pepper.

Place the joint in a roasting tray and roast in a
very hot oven (210°C) for 20 minutes or alternatively
sear in a hot pan, then turn the oven down to 55°C
and leave in overnight or for 8 hours. This method
allows the beef to cook all the way through very
evenly without over cooking.

To Serve

Slice the beef and serve with all of your favourite
vegetables, the more the merrier!

Remember to save any roasting juices for your gravy.

Yorkshire Pudding

In catering we often make this en masse and never bother with a special recipe that needs to be multiplied depending on the yield we want. Very simply we weigh the eggs we need and match the flour and milk in quantity.

The way we estimate the amount we need is as follows: at the Forge we serve huge Yorkshires so our recipe calls for 1 egg per Yorkie, at the Abbey we serve a regular size and allow half an egg per Yorkie – so it's up to you what size Yorkshire pudding you like to serve but the method remains the same.

INGREDIENTS

equal quantities of:
  eggs, milk and flour
oil or beef dripping for cooking
salt
ground white pepper

METHOD

Prep time: 5 minutes   Cook time: 25 minutes

Preheat your oven to 200°C/gas 7

Choose a Yorkshire pudding tray (at the Forge
we use large muffin trays) and add a dessert spoon
of oil or beef dripping into each well. Place the trays
in the oven to preheat.

Decide how many eggs you need then crack the eggs
into a bowl and weigh them. Now weigh out the
same amount of plain flour and whole milk.

Mix the 3 equal weights of ingredients together (you
may use a mixer for ease). Season well with salt and
ground white pepper.

Take the smoking-hot Yorkie trays out of the oven
and, as quickly and carefully as possible, pour some
mixture into each well – until just under half full.

Put the filled trays back into the oven for
25 minutes or until golden and very well risen.

These Yorkshire are delicious straight from
the oven but will freeze beautifully.

Serves 6–8

Gravy

INGREDIENTS

2.3 ltr good beef stock (shop bought is fine)

If you'd like to home make your stock:

  6 large beef bones

  2 onions

  10 carrots

  2 tins of tinned tomatoes

  1 head of celery

  1 garlic bulb

  1 sprig sage

  1 sprig rosemary

  4 bay leaves

  100g tomato purée

1 bottle red wine

6 shallots (chopped with skins)

beef trimmings

METHOD

Prep time: 5 minutes   Cook time: 4½ hours
Gravy
Prep time: 5 minutes   Cook time: 1 hour

For the Stock

Cover all of the ingredients with water, then boil in a large saucepan for 4 hours.

Pass through a sieve. Further reduce the liquid down to 4 pints (roughly 2 litres).

For the Gravy

Put the beef stock into a large pan, adding the red wine, shallots and any beef trimmings.

Simmer gently for at least an hour to reduce to approx 2 pints (1 litre) then add any roasting juices you may have.

Pass through a sieve before serving.

Real Sherry Trifle

INGREDIENTS

1 pack lady's finger biscuits
200g raspberries
150ml cream sherry
100ml raspberry coulis
1 ltr custard
1 ltr whipped cream
60g toasted almonds

METHOD

Prep time: 30 minutes   Chill time: 4 hours

Place the lady's fingers in the base of a large glass serving bowl.

Sprinkle over the raspberries and douse in the sherry and the coulis.

Carefully cover in custard.

Top with the cream and the almonds.

Allow at least 4 hours in the fridge for the sponge fingers to absorb the sherry and coulis, and go all mushy and boozy!

Table dressing

Tins of rolled cutlery; every condiment in your cupboard!
Bowls of lemon and lime; lemon balm instead of flowers.

EATING OUTSIDE

BBQing is not essential but adds lots of theatre and I just love to hang out around the warm fire long after the food bit ends.

These recipes are just as good prepared from the kitchen (which means half of the mess and effort!) but if, like me, you like to keep the 'other half' busy then get them to spark up the Barbie for this.

I know I say it in almost every chapter, but really – condiments are king on this, pull out every relish, sauce, mayo or drizzle you can find. Sometimes I even load a whole separate table for them as it really is a matter of the 'filthier' the better.

EATING OUTSIDE **WINE MATCH**

Wine time and it's a great chance to serve rosé – something about eating outside and rosé just feels right, and the fruity notes and tempting colour are always a great time to start a party.

I've opted for an English rosé as I love the sweeter notes. For the red I've matched an Italian Primitivo, juicy and really full of life, it will cut through the fat of the ribs and complement the smoke of the bbq. This red also works surprisingly well with the fish in its rich tomato sauce.

EATING OUTSIDE **COCKTAIL**

Serves 1

Watermelon Smash

This was created to use up a glut of watermelon trimmings we had from one of our summery salads. Its light, fruity taste was an instant hit with our regulars and it became a firm favourite at the Forge. It's a fab match for a BBQ as it is not overly sweet and goes really well with smoky meats

INGREDIENTS

50ml vodka
20ml honey
20ml lemon juice
fresh watermelon

To Serve

watermelon
lemon slices

METHOD

Muddle the watermelon in a medium tumbler, add the rest of the ingredients and stir.

Garnish with watermelon and lemon slices.

Serves 2–4

Smoky Sticky Ribs

INGREDIENTS

1 rack of pork ribs (extra meaty)

Rub

20g mustard seed
20g fennel seeds
20g peppercorns
20g cayenne pepper
20g garlic powder
20g onion powder
80g salt

Sauce

200ml black treacle
200g brown sugar
100ml Worcestershire sauce
500ml olive oil

To Smoke

500g woodchips (BBQ style)

METHOD

Prep time: 30 minutes   Chilling time: 6 hours
Cook time: 7 hours

To Prepare the Ribs

Create the rub: toast the spices together in a pan, then blitz in a blender to create a fine powder (this can be stored in an airtight tub and used whenever, as it will do at least 4 racks of ribs).

Create the sauce: melt the treacle, sugar and Worcestershire sauce in a pan to form a paste (this paste will also keep, and can be used for more than 1 rack of ribs).

Cover the ribs in the spice mix and refrigerate for at least 6 hours.

Remove the ribs from the fridge and rub in the sauce paste.

Smoke the ribs.

To Smoke the Ribs

Place the chips in a deep roasting pan, light them and allow them to smoulder.

Place an oven rack or old cake rack on top of them.

Place the ribs on the rack and cover with 2 layers of tin foil.

Leave to smoke for 1 hour.

To Finish

Preheat oven to 90°C/gas ¼

Place in the oven at 90°C for 6 hours or until the meat falls apart when pressed with the back of a fork.

To Serve

Serve straight away or refrigerate and steal a slice at midnight.

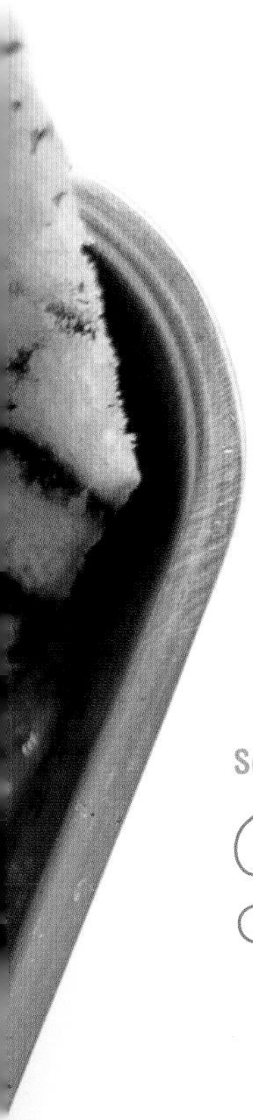

Serves 4

Fish in a Pan

INGREDIENTS

1kg white fish fillet (such as cod)
8 ripe tomatoes
1 onion (finely diced)
1 tbsp white wine vinegar
2 garlic cloves (finely chopped)
75ml white wine
olives
2 tbsp olive oil
salt and pepper to taste

To Serve

toast or garlic bread
best olive oil

METHOD

Prep time: 5 minutes   Cook time: 20 minutes

Preheat oven to 210ºC/gas 8

Take a roasting pan and lay a white fish fillet in it skin side down.

Add the fresh tomatoes, onions, vinegar, garlic, wine, salt and pepper, olives and oil.

Roast in a hot oven for about 20 minutes.

To Serve

If you're in good company then the very best way to enjoy this dish is straight from the roasting-hot pan, spooned on to toast or garlic bread, drizzled with a little fresh olive oil to finish.

Serves 4

Pomegranate Salad

INGREDIENTS

2 romaine lettuces (sliced)
1 red chilli (finely shredded)
1 pomegranate (seeds only)
1 tbsp coriander (chopped)
1 shallot (peeled and finely chopped)
salt and pepper
drizzle of olive oil
½ orange (juiced)

METHOD

Prep time: 20 minutes   Cooking time: 0 minutes

Mix all the ingredients together in a large bowl until well combined.

Serve alone or with the duck leg (pg. 52) shredded up.

Pink Slaw

INGREDIENTS

4 carrots
1 small onion
¼ red cabbage
1 tsp Dijon mustard
500g mayonnaise
salt and pepper

METHOD

Prep time: 5 minutes   Cook time: 0 minutes

Grate all the vegetables, using a medium grater, in a food processor.

Put the mixture into a bowl and then season with salt and pepper.

Add the mustard and mayonnaise and mix well until all the ingredients are combined.

Serves 6–8

Sals Corsi

INGREDIENTS

1 cucumber (grated and drained)
500g plain yoghurt (pg 42)
100ml best olive oil
1 garlic clove (finely chopped)
1 tsp dill (chopped)
freshly ground black pepper
salt to taste

To serve

toast or crunchy bread

METHOD

Prep time: 5 minutes   Cooking time: 0 minutes

Mix the all the ingredients together well and finish
with a good sprinkle of freshly ground black pepper
and a drizzle of olive oil.

To Serve

Eat alone with garlic or toasted breads, or serve
as a condiment to lamb or chicken dishes.

Serves 8

Peanut Butter Cheesecake

INGREDIENTS

1 large pack digestive biscuits
200g butter (melted)
250ml double cream
500g Philadelphia cream cheese
100g sugar
250g crunchy peanut butter
200g caramel sauce / boiled tin of condensed milk

To Serve

fresh fruit
chocolate sauce

METHOD

Prep time: 20 minutes   Chill time: 1 hour

Blitz the biscuits into a fine crumb in a food processor and then mix in the melted butter.

Press the mixture into the bottom of a 20cm (8") springform tin, then chill in the refrigerator while you create the cream cheese topping.

Whisk together the cream, Philadelphia and sugar in a kitchen mixer until stiff.

Remove the bowl from the mixer and, using your hands, squeeze in the peanut butter and caramel so as to keep some lumps within the mixture.

Take the tin out of the fridge then, still using your hands, scrape the filling into the tin and spread evenly over the biscuit base.

Chill for at least 1 hour before serving.

To Serve

Serve with fresh fruit (or chocolate sauce if you're feeling naughty).

EXQUISITE EVENING

Put simply, go wild.

You won't have gone to all this trouble over dinner to eat it out of your lap during an episode of 'Corrie', so take plenty of time setting the table (I like to do mine the night before).

Each course will need its own set of serving spoons and table cutlery and add any sauces and condiments you think your guests may enjoy.

Plan your music and lighting for the evening and have a couple of fun after-dinner games handy – my favourite part!

Table dressing

Opulence; every candlestick in the house; linen napkins and tablecloth; china and glistening glassware – a glass for each wine.

Your aperitif glasses (sherry) can be ready on a tray or an arrival table in the house where you expect guests to congregate before dinner is served.

The cheese and port can be out on display and so can the petits fours. This all adds to the ambience of the room and means that once the main course is served there is very little left to do with regards to the dinner service, so you can relax and enjoy your evening. Bread and table water are a must for this kind of occasion.

Sherry, White, Red, Port and Pudding Wine

You may have dipped into the recent foodie fashion of sherry drinking and I've always been a huge fan. I love what a fine dry sherry does for one's appetite before a meal. The salty dryness is the perfect palate cleanser and sherry really gets the juices flowing – I have picked a Manzanilla because it's just about as dry as they come, and that's just what I'm after to get people in the mood for dinner.

For the white wine I am pairing a show-stopping wine – a top-class Montrachet. I do feel that you don't really need to recommended a top-class wine, because they are all pretty amazing.

You can't go too far wrong with any wine that will set you back in excess of £50 per bottle.

On this occasion I just couldn't resist though, so here it is. Like liquid gold in a glass, so rich and almost oily, it is a shame to eat anything at all with this wine! But it is quite simply mind-blowing with the scallops in butter.

For the red I've gone for a Nuit Saint George. This burgundy wine is elegant and fine, and although it has plenty of character it is not too heavy so it's perfect for a long evening around the dinner table.

It's always lovely to have the cheese out on display on a sideboard or nearby table, and it means that the cheese will be perfectly room temperature by the time you get round to eating it. It also means you can set out the plates, knives, port and glassware so that later in the evening you can relax with guests. I have paired a Vargellas ruby port for this menu but a tawny would work just as well.

With the pudding wine I have plucked out a classic Sauternes, which is not too sweet by pudding wine standards and has enough fruit to complement the chocolates being served.

Both the port and pudding wine can be served with the cheese and petits fours and work really well with either. Lots of our clients really enjoy a sticky pudding wine with ripe room-temperature cheese and the port/chocolate combo is a real winner!

Serves 10

Goat's Cheese Panna Cotta

with Pear Relish

INGREDIENTS

Goat's Cheese Panna Cotta

1kg log of goat's cheese
1 sprig rosemary (chopped)
¼ tsp cumin
½ tsp pepper
200ml cream
4 sheets gelatine (dissolved in
    a little of the cream in a pan on the stove)

Pear Relish

½ tsp Chinese five-spice powder
100ml vinegar
75g sugar
1 stick cinnamon
6 pears (peeled and finely diced)

To Serve

best olive oil
balsamic vinegar
freshly ground black pepper

METHOD

For the Panna Cotta
Prep time: 15 minutes   Chill time: 2 hours
For the Relish
Prep time: 10 minutes   Cook time: 30 minutes

For the Panna Cotta

Peel the goat's cheese skin away, then blend the cheese in a food processor until completely smooth.

Add the rosemary, cumin and pepper, and continue to blend while adding the cream.

Finally, add the cream and gelatine mixture, then pour into a mould (loaf tin or terrine) lined with cling film.

Chill for at least 2 hours, turn the terrine out on to a chopping board and slice to serve.

For the Relish

Toast the Chinese five-spice in a pan until it becomes fragrant, then add the vinegar, sugar and cinnamon stick and stir until the sugar is all dissolved.

Add the diced pear and slowly reduce the liquids away until you're left with a sticky chutney.

If you'd like to keep the relish, then pour into a sterilized jar while still piping hot (with great caution), and put the lid on. If the seal is unbroken it should keep well for at least a year.

To Serve

Place a slice of the panna cotta onto the centre of the starter plate. Add a neat spoonful of the relish to one side of the panna cotta. Drizzle with olive oil and a little balsamic vinegar and garnish with a twist of freshly ground black pepper.

Be sure to plate them all at once, facing the same direction on the plate and putting the relish in the same spot each time. This will make for a really professional look to the start of your dinner party.

Scallops
with Hazelnut Butter

INGREDIENTS

3 scallops per person (in shell)

Hazelnut Butter

450g butter
100g roasted hazelnuts
garlic

1 lemon (juice and zest)
a pinch of black pepper
a pinch of rock salt

To Serve

parsley (freshly chopped)
lemon wedges

METHOD

Prep time: 30 minutes   Cook time: 10 minutes

For the Hazelnut Butter

Soften the butter and mix all of the ingredients together until well combined.

Roll the mixture in greaseproof paper to create a log, and chill until needed.

For the Scallops

Preheat oven to 250ºC/gas 9

Sear the scallops in a hot pan and place in their shells. Top each scallop with a slice of hazelnut butter and cook in the oven at 250ºC for 5 minutes.

To Serve

Sprinkle with fresh chopped parsley and lemon wedges and you may want to have some finger bowls at the ready!

Serves 1 per 200g fillet

Blackened Beef Fillet

Smoked Cheddar Dauphinoise,

Red Wine and Garlic Purée and Watercress,

served with Garden Greens

INGREDIENTS

Blackened Beef Fillet

200g beef fillet per person
lots of salt, pepper and oil

Jus

Gravy (pg. 88) reduced to 500ml

Smoked Cheddar Dauphinoise
Serves 10

20 large potatoes
400g smoked Cheddar cheese (grated)
150g butter
200ml double cream
300ml good chicken stock
1 sprig rosemary
salt and pepper to taste

Red Wine Garlic Purée
Serves 10

8 garlic bulbs (peeled and boiled)
500ml red wine
a pinch of salt

To Serve

watercress
your favourite green vegetables
butter

Blackened Beef Fillet

Smoked Cheddar Dauphinoise, Red Wine and Garlic Purée and Watercress, served with Garden Greens

METHOD

For the Blackened Beef Fillet:
Prep time: 10 minutes   Cook time: 1 hour

For the Smoked Cheddar Dauphinoise
Prep time: 30 minutes   Cook time: 1½ hours

For the Red Wine Garlic Purée
Prep time: 15 minutes   Cook time: 30 minutes

For the Blackened Beef Fillet

Preheat oven to 60°C/gas ¼

Season the fillet well with salt and pepper.
Sear the beef all over, until very dark on all sides, in a very hot pan with a little oil.

Cook in the oven for 1 hour at 60°C
Slice and serve – yes, it's that simple!

For the Smoked Cheddar Dauphinoise

Preheat oven to 180°C/gas 6

Line an ovenproof dish with greaseproof paper.

Peel and very thinly slice the potatoes (use a mandolin for this if you can). Cover the bottom of the dish with a couple of layers of the sliced potato, season with a little salt and pepper then sprinkle over half of the cheese.

Cover this with another layer of potatoes, then the rest of the cheese. Finally top with the last of the potato slices.

In a pan, melt the butter, cream, stock and rosemary together and season if necessary.

Pour the mixture slowly over the potatoes and allow the liquid to seep in through the gaps and sink to the bottom.

Cover the dish with a layer of baking paper and then foil and bake in the oven for around 1 hour to 1½ hours until a knife slides though the potatoes with ease.

For the Red Wine Garlic Purée

Place the boiled garlic in a pan with the wine and boil with a pinch of salt until the wine is reduced to almost nothing.

Blend in a food processor until smooth.

Add a little salt to taste.

For the Jus

Reduce gravy (pg.88), by simmering in a saucepan over a medium heat until it is reduced to 500ml.

To Serve

Warm your plates in the oven if possible. Put a spoonful of garlic purée onto the dinner plate. Using the back of your spoon, smear the purée across the plate in a circle or crescent shape.

Place a slice of the potatoes on top followed by a slice of the beef. Finish with a handful of watercress and a drizzle of jus. Serve with bowls of green vegetables in butter.

Alternatively this dish can be served at the table whole just allowing guests to help themselves!

Serves 12

Petits Fours

Chilli Fudge

INGREDIENTS

397g tin condensed milk
400g dark chocolate
200g icing sugar
1 tsp chilli flakes

METHOD

Prep time: 5 minutes   Setting time: 30 minutes

Mix the condensed milk, chocolate and icing sugar
together in a mixer to form a fudge.

Press the fudge into a 20cm (8") tin lined with
greaseproof paper.

Sprinkle over the chilli flakes and allow to set for
30 minutes.

Slice into cubes or bars to serve.

This fudge can be topped with all sorts of
things from nuts to sweeties, dried fruits and
more chocolate!

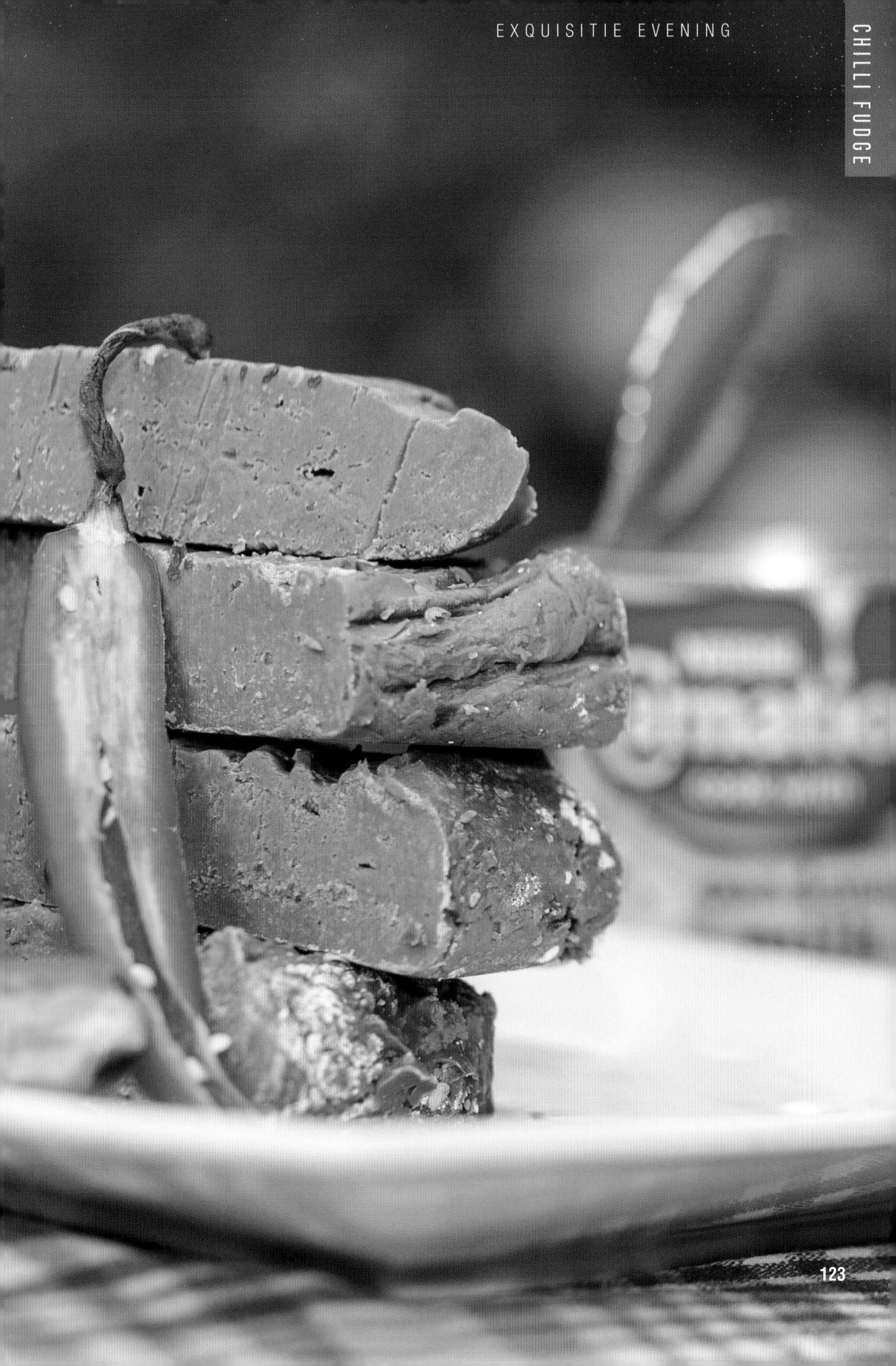

Serves 12

Petits Fours

Dark Chocolate Truffles

The amazing thing about these truffles is that you can change the base recipe into many flavours by either adding a flavour to the mix, such as orange essence or a little of your favourite liqueur, or rolling them in a coating like desiccated coconut, chopped nuts, freeze-dried fruits or cocoa powder.

This is a great cheat for a dinner party as you can make one easy batch of truffle mix and finish in several difference flavours and effects.

INGREDIENTS

300g best quality dark chocolate (at least 70%)
300g double cream
50g butter

METHOD

Prep time: 10 minutes   Setting time: 4 hours

Chop the chocolate and tip into a large bowl.
Put the cream and butter into a saucepan and heat gently until the butter melts and the cream reaches simmering point. Remove from heat, and then pour over the chocolate.

Stir the chocolate and cream together until you have a smooth mixture. Add any flavourings to the truffle mix at this stage – divide the mixture between bowls and mix in liqueurs or other flavourings, a teaspoon at a time, to taste. Try bourbon, Grand Marnier, coconut rum or the zest and juice of an orange – or leave plain.

Cool and chill for at least 4 hours

When cool you can shape your truffles into balls and coat with cocoa powder or different things.

Keep in the fridge in an airtight container for a week or freeze and use whenever needed. These make a great addition to afternoon tea!

Cheeseboard

Old School

PREPARING A CHEESEBOARD

So many cheeses so little time! When preparing a well-balanced cheeseboard it is important to try and consider the different types of cheese and the milk used in the cheese itself.

I always try to have at least one cheese from each category of cheese:

Soft
Brie, cream cheeses, many goat's cheeses.

Semi-soft
Gubbeen and softer English cheese such as Sharpham's.

Hard
Cheddars and Swiss cheeses.

Blue
Stiltons are great but there are so many different types of blue cheese: blue sheep's cheese is amazing (Lanark Blue) and blue Brie – so creamy! See if you can showcase something different.

Washed rind
My favourite – the smelly ones that have their rinds washed in all sorts from milk to spirits and even champagne, and usually result in the really pungent cheeses like Stinking Bishop.

And mix those up with the different milks used:

Cow

Goat

Sheep

Three milk (cow, goat and sheep)

Make sure there is a real range of cheeses on offer.

It is most important to offer a couple of relishes and my personal favourite is a quince jelly. These don't have to be homemade.

Always have butter and biscuits at the ready and fruits such as grapes and figs add another layer to the course. Cheese is very good with dark chocolate so try the truffles together with a little blue cheese and port – amazing!

When I prepare for a special event that calls for a cheeseboard, it is always my first job – that way I can set it out in plenty of time to allow it to come up to room temperature and get all gooey and delicious.

The rights of Sarah Xhumrri and Sara Donaldson to be identified as the authors of this work have been asserted in accordance with the Copyright Act 1991.

No part of this publication may be reproduced, stored in a retrieval system or transmitted in any form or by any means, electronic, mechanical, photocopying, recording or otherwise, without prior permission in writing from the publisher.

Lily Publications and the restaurants included in this publication accept no responsibility for any injury or allergic reactions resulting from the recipes, or the ingredients contained therein, enclosed in this publication.

To the best of our knowledge, all recipes illustrated are correct and to the standards required. Neither Lily Publications nor the restaurants included in this publication accept any liability for any misuse or neglect. All care and attention should be made to hygiene in food preparation and it is advised that the best quality ingredients should used to obtain the best results. Special attention should be given where a manufacturer's goods give specific instructions on preparation and the oven or grill should be pre-heated to the specified temperature.

Oven temperatures given are for fan-assisted ovens. We recommend using an oven thermometer. If using a non fan-assisted oven, adjust temperatures according to the manufacturer's instructions.

ISBN: 978-1-911177-28-9
Published by **Lily Publications Ltd.**, PO Box 33, Ramsey, Isle of Man, IM99 4LP
Tel: +44 (0)1624 898446, Fax: +44 (0)1624 898449 www.lilypublications.co.uk lilypubs@manx.net

Printed by Gomer Press